the guide to owning a
Hedgehog

Audrey Pavia

T.F.H. Publications, Inc.
One TFH Plaza
Third and Union Avenues
Neptune City, NJ 07753

Library of Congress Cataloging-in-Publication Data
Pavia, Audrey.
The guide to owning a hedgehog / Audrey Pavia.
p. cm.
ISBN 0-7938-2225-4 (alk. paper)
I. Title.
SF459.H43P38 2003
636.9'332--dc22
2003020025

Printed and bound in USA

www.tfh.com

Contents

Hedgehogs are best known for their quills. The average "hedgie" has about 5,000 quills that measure around one inch long.

THE GUIDE TO OWNING A HEDGEHOG

Introducing the Hedgehog

The hedgehog is a fascinating and unusual animal with a long natural history and an interesting human-related past. With their smiling expressions—accompanied by a curious nature—hedgehogs have charmed many pet

The two species of hedgehog most often seen in North America are the African Hedgehog and the Algerian Hedgehog. Many pet "hedgies" are a cross between the two.

Hedgehogs have powerful legs. Although they usually walk slowly, they can run about 6.5 feet per second.

owners. Once a "hedgie" bonds with you, they say, you will be friends for life.

HEDGEHOG FACTS

Fourteen different species of hedgehogs can be found in the world. The most commonly known hedgehog in the world is the European hedgehog, a creature that has inspired considerable lore throughout the Western world. The two species of hedgehog most often seen in captivity in North America are the African Hedgehog (*Atelerix albiventris*, also known by some as the African Pygmy Hedgehog), and the Algerian Hedgehog. These species are nearly identical in appearance and hard to tell apart. Many pet hedgehogs are actually a cross between these two species.

Hedgehogs are mammals in the Insectivora order, making them relatives of shrews and moles. Hedgehogs have been around since the time of the dinosaurs and have changed very little since then.

The average African Hedgehog weighs between one-half and one and a quarter pounds and is 5 to 8 inches long. About the size of a guinea pig and sometimes smaller, hedgehogs have round ears, round eyes, and a pointed snout. Most hedgehogs can live to about four to seven years of age in captivity.

Hedgehogs in North America are found in a variety of colors, including albino, cinnacot (pink skin and peach and tan quills bands), and salt and pepper (black skin and dark brown and black banded quills), to name just a few.

HEDGEHOGS IN THE WILD

Domestic hedgehogs retain the same instincts and physical traits of their wild ancestors, so understanding the behavior of wild hedgehogs is crucial to your appreciation of a pet hedgehog.

Hedgehogs are best known for their quills, which are sharp spines attached to the skin that serve as a defensive device when faced with predators. The average hedgehog has about 5,000 quills measuring approximately an inch long. Baby hedgehogs are born with their quills under the skin to avoid damaging the mother hedgehog's birth canal. The quills then surface through the skin when the hedgehog reaches a few days of age.

Hedgehogs have powerful legs that enable them to dig for insects and run quickly to escape predators. Although they usually walk slowly, hedgehogs are capable of running about 6.5 feet per second. Their claws are strong for digging, and their feet have five toes each.

Hedgehogs have strong, sharp teeth designed to help them catch and chew on insects. They have from 36 to 44 teeth, with upper and lower first incisors larger than the rest.

The old myth about hedgehogs mating face to face is untrue. Male hedgehogs breed with female hedgehogs in the same way dogs, cats, and other mammals do, with the male mounting the female to deposit his sperm in her

Depending on the species, female hedgies can give birth to 1 to 10 young. The babies are weaned between six and seven weeks of age.

The wild hedgehog's diet consists mostly of insects, though he will occasionally eat seeds, berries and fruit.

vaginal canal. During the mating process, the female flattens her spines to allow the male to proceed unharmed.

Experts believe that, after mating, the male and female go their separate ways, and the female raises the young alone. She builds a nest of dried plant material in a safe place (either in a burrow or above the ground, depending on the species) and gives birth to 1 to 10 young, depending on the species. The young are born hairless, with their ears and eyes closed.

Baby hedgehogs are weaned between six and seven weeks of age. By this time, they have fur, and their quills have developed so they are able to hunt insects on their own.

The wild hedgehog's diet consists mostly of insects, primarily crickets, earthworms, beetles, millipedes, slugs, and caterpillars. Wild hedgehogs will also scavenge the remains of dead animals and eat eggs and young found in birds' nests. Occasionally they will eat seeds, berries, and fruit. African Hedgehogs have even been known to eat scorpions and small poisonous snakes with no ill effects.

Hedgehogs are considered diurnal, which means they are active mainly during the day. However, most hedgehog owners have discovered that hedgehogs do most of their eating and exercising at night.

Predators, such as hawks, eagles, and wild dogs, hunt hedgehogs in their natural environment. Hedgehogs protect themselves by contracting a small muscle at the base of each spine to make them erect. Hedgehogs will often first erect their spines and wait for danger to pass. If the danger persists, the hedgehog will curl up into a ball. This allows him to protect his delicate under-parts from attack. The tighter the hedgehog curls, the more his spines protrude. Most predators are reluctant to take a bite out of such a spiny meal and will move on to easier prey.

HEDGEHOGS AND HUMANS

Hedgehogs and humans have an interesting, related past. In China, hedgehogs are sacred and never harmed. The hedgehog has also played a part in Western culture, as is evidenced by the celebration of Groundhog Day February 2. Although we currently use groundhogs and their shadows in a ceremony to predict spring's arrival, the original weather forecaster was the hedgehog.

Originally, the ancient Romans waited to see if the hedgehog saw his shadow and, if he did, it meant that six more weeks of winter remained. When the tradition arrived in North America, the duty of forecasting the arrival of spring eventually fell to the groundhog because at the time there were no hedgehogs in this part of the world.

Hedgehogs have not always been revered for their forecasting talents. Farmers in medieval Britain falsely accused hedgehogs of stealing milk from their cows in the middle of the night. As a result, a bounty was put on the heads of hedgehogs and many of

Long before the American tradition of Goundhog Day, the ancient Romans used hedgehogs to predict the arrival of spring.

the animals were needlessly slaughtered.

THE HEDGEHOG AS A PET

Although people have admired hedgehogs for centuries, hedgehogs didn't become an official part of the pet trade until the early 1990s.

The story begins in 1991 in Nigeria, where hedgehogs were reportedly overpopulating one part of the country. Boxes of hedgehogs were given to shippers who, in turn, sent a few thousand of these animals to New York City to be sold as pets.

By 1993, hedgehogs had become a fad pet in the US. Between 1991 and 1994, about 80,000 hedgehogs were shipped from Nigeria to New York. The United States Department of Agriculture banned further imports when Nigeria was stricken with an outbreak of hoof and mouth disease.

By then, however, hedgehogs had become a popular pet, and profiteers were selling breeding pairs for as much as $6,000. Prohibitive costs led to extensive inbreeding, which brought out genetic diseases in some of the hedgehogs.

In 1997, a registry was formed to help breeders recognize and promote quality bloodlines. Today, the International Hedgehog Association in Divide, Colorado owns this registry and has approximately 12,000 hedgehogs on record.

SHOULD YOU GET A HEDGEHOG?

Hedgehogs are cute, usually easygoing, and don't make huge demands on your time and attention. However, a hedgie requires daily care, handling, and exercise to stay happy and healthy, and he may not be the perfect match for every member of your family.

Care

You can expect to spend time handling your hedgehog (at least several minutes per day), feeding him (twice a day), changing his water, and giving him at least two hours of exercise per day, either outside of his cage or on an exercise wheel in his cage. You'll also need to remove soiled bedding and litter every day and clean out the entire cage once a week. In addition, if your hedgehog becomes ill, you'll have to take him to the vet. You'll also have to make sure that the temperature in your home doesn't go below 70°F because hedgehogs cannot tolerate temperatures below this level.

If you want to bring a hedgehog into your home, you should ask yourself the following questions:

• Are you willing to take responsibility for a hedgehog and his needs for the next three to seven years, whether you move, change jobs, or have a new baby?

• Do you have the time, money, and patience for a hedgehog?

• If your hedgehog becomes ill, will you take him to a veterinarian?

• Do you have the time to give your hedgehog the attention and exercise he needs?

• Are you willing to take on a pet that is not trainable like a dog but instead has his own unique characteristics?

•When you are away from home, will you be able to find someone to care for your hedgehog? You can leave him overnight with a supply of food and water, but if he must be alone longer, someone should attend to his needs.

Handling a Hedgehog

Hedgehogs require regular handling to bond with humans. They are most active at night but are amenable to handling in the morning and at dusk. They sometimes nip or bite, and they are covered with quills that can cause moderate pain to an unwary owner. Some hedgehog owners wear gloves to handle their hedgies, but others maintain that you should never wear gloves when handling your pet, especially because gloves are not allowed at most hedgehog shows.

Allergies

Before you add a hedgehog to the family, consider the possibility that you may have a slight allergic reaction when handling this pet.

Most people who are allergic to dogs, cats, or other mammals are usually not allergic to hedgehogs. However, some people experience a skin reaction when they hold a hedgehog in their hands. Experts believe this is due to coming in contact with the animal's spines. Hedgehogs "anoint"

Although people have admired them for centuries, hedgehogs became an official part of the pet trade as recently as the 1990s.

their spines with saliva. When a spine touches human skin, the saliva may cause an allergic reaction at the spot.

Hedgehogs and Children

Because hedgehogs are small and somewhat delicate, they should not be handled by children younger than the age of seven. Also, hedgehogs tend to make soft vocalizations, mostly at night, and they make other noises at night while playing in their cages. A child could be awakened at night if the hedgehog's cage is in or near her room.

Hedgehogs and Other Pets

Before you bring home a hedgehog, think about your other pets, especially if you have a dog, cat, or a large bird such as a parrot. It's important to note that, in the wild, larger animals hunt hedgehogs. Hedgehogs who live in captivity are still leery of predators and will be stressed by constant encounters with large pets.

HEDGEHOG PROOFING

Hedgehogs do best when they receive a couple of hours of exercise a day outside of the cage. Because hedgehogs are so small, it's best to let them roam in a small confined room, such as a bathroom. You will have to "hedgehog proof" any room before letting your pet run loose. This means eliminating all holes and spaces where your hedgehog might hide and locating and removing all items that he could reach and chew, including telephone cords and electrical wires.

LEGALITY

Another important issue you need to consider is whether hedgehogs are legal where you live. As of this writing, it is illegal to keep hedgehogs as pets in California, Arizona, Georgia, Vermont, Pennsylvania, Hawaii, and in several counties and cities in other states. If hedgehogs are illegal where you live, you will be breaking the law if you acquire one of these pets.

MEET A HEDGIE, LOVE A HEDGIE

The best way to get to know a hedgehog is to live with one. Hedgehogs are cute, interesting, and entertaining. Hedgehog owners enjoy watching their pets' antics, including the hedgehog's tendency to "anoint" himself by rubbing foamy saliva all over his quills. And, because hedgehogs are such good hunters, many owners also enjoy watching them chasing down and eating insects.

If you've never interacted with a hedgehog, it's a good idea to spend some time with one before you embark on ownership. You can do this by offering to provide a foster home for a hedgehog through a hedgehog rescue group, or you can offer to pet-sit a hedgehog for a friend who owns one of these creatures. By "borrowing" a hedgehog for a short time, you'll get a good sense of what it would be like to own one.

Selecting Your Hedgehog

If you have done your research and decided that a hedgehog is the right pet for you, your next step is to locate one of these fascinating creatures.

You can opt to get your hedgehog in one of several ways: from a pet store, breeder, or hedgehog rescue group.

Wherever you find your hedgehog, don't be afraid to look around and visit more than one animal. Check out several different hedgehogs before you decide which one will be your beloved pet. Remember that hedgehogs have a lifespan of four to seven years, so be prepared to care for your pet for the rest of his life.

PET SHOPS

Like most people who are fond of hedgehogs, you probably first saw one of these little animals in a pet shop. If a pet shop seems like the best option for you, buy your hedgehog only from a store that keeps the animals in a clean environment, and be certain the animals look healthy. Don't buy a hedgehog from a store where these animals are kept in dirty, smelly cages.

Avoid animals that have runny noses, unclear eyes, or diarrhea. Make sure the shop gives you a health guarantee that allows you to return the hedgehog within a period of time if the animal becomes ill. After buying your hedgehog, take your new pet to a veterinarian to make sure he's healthy.

BUYING FROM A BREEDER

Another option for acquiring a hedgehog is buying from a breeder. People who breed hedgehogs do so in order to show them and sell them as pets.

Responsible breeders are caring individuals who take good care of their hedgehogs, know a lot about the species, and socialize young hedgehogs so they will make better pets. A responsible breeder also cares about the health of his or her hedgehogs and should be willing to take a hedgehog back if you decide you can't keep him.

Buying from a responsible breeder is also a good idea because you'll have someone you can go to with questions about how to care for your pet. Most breeders are more than willing to answer questions and provide advice about how to care for hedgehogs.

Before you decide to buy a hedgehog from a particular breeder, make sure to ask some important questions to help determine if the breeder is responsible:

• How many hedgehogs does the breeder own?

• How long has he or she bred hedgehogs?

• Has the breeder ever seen any health problems in his or her stock, especially Wobbly Hedgehog Syndrome (WHS), a debilitating neurological condition indicated by a wobbly gait?

Also, ask if you can visit the breeder's facilities. You need to see that the breeder's animals are healthy and that the facility is clean and well kept.

Expect a responsible hedgehog breeder to ask you some questions, too. He or she may want to know if

Age is one factor to consider when searching for a hedgehog as a new pet. If you want a baby hedgie, make sure you get one that is at least six weeks old.

THE GUIDE TO OWNING A HEDGEHOG

Wherever you find your new hedgehog—in a pet shop, at a breeder's, or in a rescue facility—check out several hedgies before you decide which one will be your pet.

A healthy hedgehog's ears and nose are clean and free of discharge, while his eyes are wide and alert, the fur on his belly is soft and free of mats, and there are no bare patches among his quills.

you've ever had a hedgehog before, if you know much about hedgehog care, and other questions about how you plan to keep your pet.

To find a local hedgehog breeder, look on the Internet for breeder websites. Local veterinarians who specialize in treating exotics may also know of a breeder. If you are lucky, a local 4-H club will have a hedgehog project and will be able to refer you to breeders in your area.

If you want to buy a hedgehog from a breeder but can't find one locally, you may be able to find a breeder in another part of the country who might be willing to ship a hedgehog to you via air. Be aware that shipping a hedgehog can be expensive.

RESCUING A HEDGEHOG

You also may consider adopting a hedgehog in need of a home. Like dogs, cats and other pets, hedgehogs often find themselves homeless and in need of a new family. Usually nothing is wrong with these hedgehogs; they just had the misfortune of ending up with owners who grew tired of them or who didn't realize the responsibility of taking care of a small pet.

A number of hedgehog breeders and fanciers around the country have put together hedgehog rescue

It's exciting to add a new pet to the family—especially one as interesting as a hedgehog. Closely supervise interactions between your hedgehog and pets you may already have.

groups, special groups that ask local animal control officials to notify them whenever a hedgehog enters an animal shelter. The groups take hedgehogs out of shelters, place them in foster homes, and search for permanent homes for them. Hedgehog rescue groups also take in hedgehogs from various other situations that have rendered them homeless.

The hardest part about adopting a hedgehog is finding a hedgehog rescue group in your area. Not all areas of the country are serviced by hedgehog rescue groups because hedgehogs are simply not that common. If you are fortunate enough to have a hedgehog rescue group in your area, you can find it in a number of different ways.

One of the easiest ways to locate a hedgehog rescue group is through the Internet. Type the words "hedgehog rescue" in your favorite search engine, and you'll get a list of hedgehog rescue groups around the country. You may have to visit each website to determine which group is closest to you. If you can't find one locally, consider contacting the nearest group. The group may be able to work out a way to deliver a rescued hedgehog to your home.

You could also consider contacting your local animal shelter or a veterinarian in your area who treats exotic pets for a reference to a local hedgehog rescue group. You'll also find help in locating a hedgehog rescue group in your area in the Resources section of this book.

If you plan to adopt a hedgehog from a rescue group, be prepared to answer questions about where you plan to keep your pet, what you will feed him, and other questions related to how you will care for your new hedgie. Hedgehog rescuers work hard to find good homes for the hedgehogs they take in, and they want to be sure each person who adopts a hedgehog knows how to care for these exotic animals.

The hedgehog rescue group you work with may ask you to pay a small adoption fee that will help to offset the costs of caring for homeless hedgehogs. This is money well spent, as it will be used to help other hedgies in need.

FACTORS TO CONSIDER

When searching for a hedgehog as a pet, certain important factors should be taken into consideration.

Age

The first factor to consider is the hedgehog's age. Hedgehogs usually live to be anywhere from four to seven years old. If you want to have your hedgehog for a long time, choose a younger animal. Young hedgehogs are likely to bond with you more quickly than an older hedgehog.

If you don't mind having your

It's advisable to check a hedgehog's walk. Look for a steady shuffle. A wobbly or unsteady gait could indicate illness.

hedgehog for a shorter period of time, you can get an older pet. Older hedgehogs are often in need of good homes, so it's an act of kindness to take a mature hedgehog into your home. With time and patience, you can socialize an older but possibly un-socialized hedgehog with you and other humans. Many older hedge-hogs are already strongly bonded to people and so make wonderful pets.

If you want a baby hedgehog, make sure you get one that is at least six weeks old. Taking a hedgehog at a younger age is a bad idea because the baby is too young to leave its mother.

Health

Another important factor to consid-er when buying or adopting a hedge-hog is the health of the animal you are considering. When determining a hedgehog's health, consider the fol-lowing factors.

• The hedgehog's ears and nose should be clean and free of discharge.

• The eyes should be wide and alert.

• The fur on his belly should be soft and free of mats.

• Make certain no bare patches exist through his forest of quills. Keep an eye out for scabs and parasites, such as fleas and mites.

• Be sure to take a look around the hedgehog's cage to make sure no diarrhea is present. Observe how the hedgehog walks, and look for a steady shuffle. The animal should not seem wobbly or unsteady.

• Check out the hedgehog's attitude. He should be alert and curious. A hedgehog that seems depressed and listless even after you try to interact with him may be sick. (Be aware that a sleepy hedgehog may be a bit groggy. Give him a chance to wake up.)

• Check to make sure the hedgehogs in the vicinity look healthy too. Even one sick hedgehog in close proximity can be bad news for the pet you are considering.

Temperament

If you are like most pet owners, you want an animal you can interact with. To get an idea of whether the hedgehog you are considering is well socialized, handle him to see how he reacts. Determine how long it takes him to unroll from a protective ball posture. Hissing is to be expected since the hedgehog doesn't know you, but if he clicks at you, he is threatening to bite. An aggressive hedgehog will take a lot longer to tame and may never grow to appreciate human contact.

Overall, look for a hedgehog that is curious, friendly and/or playful. You can't expect a hedgehog to come running to greet if you if he doesn't know you, but he should show some interest if he will be a good, social pet.

Gender

Gender is another consideration when choosing a hedgehog. Fortunately, both male and female hedgehogs make equally good pets, so you don't need to concern yourself with the sex of the hedgehog you like best.

You can tell the difference between a male and a female hedgehog by turning the animal over on its back. The genitals on a female are next to the anus. On a male hedgehog, the penis sheath is more toward the center of the belly.

It's important to remember that hedgehogs are solitary animals and prefer to live alone. If you put a male and female together, they will breed, and you'll be stuck with trying to find homes for a litter of hedgehogs.

WHEN YOUR PET ARRIVES

It's exciting to add a new pet to the family, especially one as interesting as a hedgehog. Everyone in the family will be anxious to touch his quills and hold him in their hands, but it's best to give your pet a few days to settle into his new surroundings before you begin handling him.

Don't be surprised if, in the beginning, your hedgehog hisses and rolls himself into a ball when you approach him. This reaction is normal for a hedgehog in new surroundings with people he doesn't know. Eventually, he will relax and come to know you and other members of your family. You can help him adjust to his new life by giving him plenty of patience and understanding. Stop by his cage often and talk to him, and provide him with food and water. In

To get an idea of whether the hedgehog you are considering is well socialized, handle him to see how he reacts, and determine how long it takes him to unroll from a protective ball posture.

time, he'll realize you are a friend, not a foe.

If you have kids, this is a good time to teach them how to behave around their new pet. Most children understand the concept of fear, and if you tell your child that the hedgehog is feeling a little afraid in his new surroundings and needs quiet time, your child will most likely respond.

Most kids can't wait to show a new hedgehog to their friends. Wait a day or two before allowing your children to invite their friends over to see your hedgehog, then limit the visits to one or two friends at a time. A room full of excited children will no

doubt frighten your hedgehog even further.

Remember that hedgehogs should not be handled by very young children but only by older kids who have been taught how to properly hold them. A child can easily be pricked by a hedgehog spine—a sensation that is bound to bring tears.

Once you are certain your older child knows how to properly handle the hedgehog, supervise to make certain the handling is being done correctly.

If you have other pets, particularly dogs, keep them away from your new hedgehog, at least for awhile. Hedgehogs are good at defending themselves with their quills, but there is no need to stress your new pet further by exposing him to a dog.

MORE THAN ONE

While some experts recommend keeping hedgehogs by themselves, others report that you can house female hedgehogs together. In fact, female hedgehogs often live in large groups at rescue facilities and get along famously.

If you plan to have more than one hedgehog, your best bet is to get only females. Get littermates if you can because they are most likely to get along. If the two females are strangers, you must introduce them slowly to one another, especially if they are older.

Your first step should be to place each hedgehog in a separate cage and put the cages side-by-side. Keep the cages together until all signs of aggression from either one of the occupants have ceased.

After your hedgehogs have spent a week living peacefully as next-door neighbors, you can try putting the more aggressive hedgie into the other's cage. This will discourage the dominant hedgehog from feeling that he has to protect his territory.

Make sure you stay in the room for most of the day to make sure the hedgies don't fight. If they do, you'll need to separate them and try it again a few days later.

Both male and female hedgehogs make equally good pets, so you don't need to concern yourself with the sex of the hedgehog you like best.

THE GUIDE TO OWNING A HEDGEHOG

Some experts recommend keeping hedgehogs by themselves, but others say that female hedgehogs can be housed together, especially if they're littermates.

If the fighting continues when you reintroduce the two hedgehogs to one another, try switching their cages. Leave each in the other's cage for a few hours. This will give them a chance to get used to each other's scent.

Once the hedgehogs seem to be getting along, move both of them into a new cage with fresh bedding, food, dishes, and other accessories. The key is to have them living together in a cage that is neutral territory, free from the scent of either hedgehog.

If you find that, after weeks of trying, your hedgehogs refuse to get along, don't push the issue any further. Some hedgies can never be friends, and forcing them together could be disastrous. Hedgehogs can and will fight and are capable of inflicting terrible wounds on one another. In fact, it's not unheard of for hedgehogs to fight to the death.

If your hedgehogs don't get along, keep them in separate cages and never put them together, even during free-run time. If you had a return agreement with the breeder, pet shop, or rescue group where you adopted your second hedgehog, you may want to consider taking the hedgie back and bringing home a different individual.

Buy the largest cage that you can afford and that will fit into your home. Your pet will appreciate as much space as you can give him.

THE GUIDE TO OWNING A HEDGEHOG

Housing Your Hedgehog

One of the most important things you can do for your hedgehog is give him a nice, well-equipped, comfortable place to live. Prepare your new pet's housing before he comes home, so you'll be prepared to let him start settling in the first day he arrives.

Make sure your hedgehog's cage has solid flooring. Hedgehogs' feet and legs can become caught in a wire-bottom cage. This enclosure should have a screen top.

THE CAGE

The cage you provide for your hedge-hog will be his source of security. You can buy a cage suitable for a hedge-hog from a pet-supply store, through a catalog that sells items for small animals, or over the Internet.

Purchase the largest cage you can afford and that will fit comfortably in your home. Hedgehogs roam quite a bit while hunting in the wild, and your pet will appreciate as much space as you can give him.

The best cage for your hedgehog will be made of wire. Wire cages allow the most air circulation, and therefore provide the best ventilation. The dimensions should add up to at least 2 square feet of floor space. The cage should have a secure top.

The next-best enclosure for a hedge-hog is an aquarium. A 20-gallon aquarium is large enough for a hedgehog. Make sure you have a secure screen top—you don't want any animals to get into your hedgehog's enclosure or for your hedgehog to get out, but you do need to allow for good ventilation.

Make certain your hedgehog cage has solid flooring. Hedgehogs' feet and legs can become easily caught and broken in a wire-bottom cage.

When choosing a cage for your hedgehog, avoid cages that open from the side. For security reasons, use a cage that has the cage door on

In the wild, hedgehogs exercise by hunting prey. Placing an exercise wheel in your hedgie's cage will ensure that he gets the exercise he needs.

It's a good idea to let your pet use ceramic crock-style food bowls that are too heavy for him to tip over, and that are easy to keep clean.

the top so you can lift your hedgehog out from the top part of the cage.

Hedgehogs have delicate legs, so the wire-mesh grid size on the sides of the cage you buy should be no more than 1 by 2 inches. Anything larger will pose a hazard to your hedgehog's safety because his legs may get caught in the wire.

MUST-HAVE CAGE ACCESSORIES

Hedgehogs need certain accessories inside their cages for optimum health and comfort. In the wild, hedgehogs get a lot of exercise because they spend a lot of time seeking and hunting prey. In order to provide your pet with adequate exercise in the confines of a cage, put an exercise wheel in his cage.

An exercise wheel is one of the most important items you can provide for your hedgehog. Hedgies with access to exercise wheels have the opportunity to run to their heart's content. They don't seem to mind that they don't get anywhere. The sheer act of running seems to make them happy.

The safest exercise wheel for a hedgehog is one made from solid material, so the hedgie's feet and legs don't get caught in wire. A wheel that measures about 11 inches in diameter is good for most hedgehogs. The wheel should have a solid or mesh-covered floor to prevent your hedgehog's feet from slipping through when he's running.

You can purchase one of these at a pet-supply store that sells products for small animals or order one through a catalog or on the Internet. You can leave your hedgehog's wheel in his cage all the time, 24 hours a day. He can then take a spin on it whenever he wishes. Look the wheel over regularly to make sure it's in good working order and be sure to wash it when you do your weekly cage cleaning.

You should also buy or make a hide box for your hedgehog. A hide box is a place where your pet can sleep and huddle for security when he needs it. You can buy a hide box from a pet-supply retailer. Make sure to get one that is made from strong, untreated wood. You can also make your own hide box, being careful to use untreated wood. An even less-expensive hide box can be made from an empty tissue box or shoebox with one side cut out.

Your hedgehog will need a food bowl. Heavy, ceramic crock-style bowls work best for hedgehogs because they are more difficult to tip over. They are also easier to keep clean than plastic or metal. Purchase one that is shallow enough to allow your pet to reach into it without struggling.

If you prefer, you can use a plastic or metal cup that attaches to the side of your hedgehog's cage. Again, make certain the cup is not too deep for your hedgehog and secure it at a low level in the cage so your pet can reach it easily.

Your hedgie needs fresh water every day in order to stay healthy. The best way to provide water is through a gravity water bottle. These bottles, available from pet-supply retailers, are usually glass and hang from the side of the cage. A metal ball inside the tip of the bottle keeps water from spilling out onto the cage,

You may also want to provide your hedgehog with some cage toys to play

Hedgehogs like to nest, and do best with clean bedding in the form of aspen or pine shavings, pelleted hay, or recycled paper bedding.

The Nylabone® Fold-Away Pet Carrier can come in handy if you have to confine your pet while cleaning his cage or taking him to the vet.

with. Many hedgies are very playful and will appreciate a solid rubber ball, children's toy trucks, toilet paper or paper towel tubes, and commercially made cat toys.

If you are fortunate enough to own a hedgehog that is amenable to litter box training, consider purchasing a small corner litter box for your pet's cage. Because hedgehogs often eliminate in one spot of the cage, take note of where this spot is located and place the litter box there in the hope that your hedgehog will get the message. For litter, you can use dust-free, non-clumping cat litter.

BEDDING

Hedgehogs like to nest, and they appreciate clean bedding to help them feel cozy. Hedgehogs do best with aspen or pine shavings, pelleted hay, or recycled paper bedding, all available from pet-supply retailers. A number of hedgehog experts recommend staying away from cedar bedding because they believe it could be hazardous to the hedgehog's lungs and respiratory health. Some experts also believe corn cob bedding can be dangerous if the hedgehog ingests it.

Place the hedgehog's bedding inside his hide box so he can snuggle up with it. It may end up all over the cage in time, so don't be surprised.

TRAVEL CARRIER

Besides the cage items listed above, you might consider purchasing a small travel carrier for your hedgehog. A travel carrier can come in handy if you have to confine your hedgehog while cleaning his cage, taking him to the vet, or moving him

Hedgehogs prefer a temperature of around 70° F. Avoid letting your hedgie's environment drop below this level because cold air encourages hedgehogs to hibernate, which can be dangerous to your pet.

for any other reason. Pet-supply retailers that sell products for small animals usually carry a selection of small animal carriers, like the Nylabone® Fold-Away Pet Carrier. Be sure to choose one that is secure and provides for adequate ventilation. Make certain your hedgie has room to turn around inside the carrier.

If you plan to travel on an airplane with your hedgehog, be sure to purchase a carrier that has been approved by the International Animal Travel Association (IATA). These carriers—which include the Nylabone® Fold-Away Pet Carrier—have been determined to have the safest construction for air travel and should carry a label that they are IATA-approved.

CAGE LOCATION

Now that you know what your hedge-hog needs in the way of accommodations, you'll want to figure out where to keep his cage.

Keep in mind that hedgehogs prefer a temperature of around 70°F. Avoid letting your hedgehog's environment drop below this temperature because cold air encourages a hedgehog to hibernate. Because the African Hedgehog species is not meant to hibernate, this situation can be dangerous and should be avoided.

Therefore, make sure your hedgehog's cage is located in a draft-free place in your home where the temperature will not go above or below 70°F. The cage should also be kept away from heat sources like furnaces, stoves, and radiators, and should not be subjected to direct sunlight. On the other hand, don't keep the cage in darkness, either.

When choosing a place for your hedgie's cage, keep in mind that hedgehogs are often most active after the sun goes down. Your pet may make a lot of noise in the middle of the night, so if you are a light sleeper, consider keeping his cage out of your bedroom at night.

It's a good idea to place your hedgehog's cage in an area of the house that is frequented by people, but that isn't the noisiest room in the house, either. A den, living room, or family room is suitable unless a lot of loud gatherings take place in that part of the house. Too much noise will make your hedgehog overly nervous and afraid to come out of his hide box.

CLEANING TIPS

Keeping your hedgehog's cage clean is very important. Unclean cages are often the cause of bacterial infections in small pets.

You should plan to clean up after your hedgehog every day. Empty out his litter box, rinse it out, and replace it with fresh litter. Wash out his water bottle and food bowl. Replace soiled bedding with fresh bedding, being sure to check inside the hide box.

Once a week, you should clean the entire cage with a mild bleach solution (a bucket of water with a splash of bleach), and let it dry out in the sun. This will help destroy bacteria and other potential pests.

It's very important to keep your hedgie's cage clean. Unclean cages are often the cause of bacterial infections in small animals.

TRAVEL ACCOMMODATIONS

Many hedgehog owners become so attached to their hedgehogs that they want to travel with them. This is not always a good idea. If you need to transport your pet to the veterinarian or to your new home, then you shouldn't hesitate to put your hedgehog in his carrier with some bedding and move onward.

However, if you are thinking of taking your hedgehog along on vacation or just for a ride, it's probably not a good idea because hedgehogs are sensitive, and feel insecure in unfamiliar surroundings. If you must travel with your pet, keep him in his travel carrier at all times. Not only will this work to keep him safe, but it will also lend him a feeling of security.

If you travel in the car with your hedgehog, make sure the air conditioner is on, especially if the car temperature exceeds 80 F. Do not leave the carrier exposed to prolonged periods of direct sunlight because of the heat. If you stop for a break, leave your hedgehog in his carrier. Not only will it frighten him to be taken out in strange surroundings, but it will also increase your chances of losing him forever if he gets away from you.

Never leave your hedgehog inside a parked car during the day, even if the windows are rolled down. Car interiors become incredibly hot in a very short period of time. The rising temperature could quickly kill your hedgehog.

If your road trip calls for an overnight stay in a hotel, plan ahead and make reservations at hotels that allow pets. While in the motel room, keep your hedgehog inside his carrier when you can't supervise him, and only let him out of his cage in the bathroom with the door closed. This is to prevent him from escaping.

Airplane rides are not recommended for hedgehogs unless necessary to move the hedgehog to a new residence. If you plan on flying somewhere and are returning, it's best to leave your hedgehog in the care of a friend or pet-sitter.

If you need to fly with your pet because of a move, make your plane reservation far in advance. Most airlines only allow two animals per cabin on an airplane, and you should transport your hedgehog under the seat in front of you, not in the safe-but-distant cargo hold. (Many airlines will not allow hedgehogs to fly in the cabin, so you may have no choice.)

If you are traveling to another state, make sure hedgehogs are legal there before you attempt to bring your pet on an airplane. Get a health certificate from a veterinarian ten days before your trip, so you know your pet is healthy, and so you can meet airline requirements.

When you are traveling, remember to bring along everything your hedgehog will need. This includes a supply of his regular food, his water bottle, fresh bedding, and fresh litter that can

THE GUIDE TO OWNING A HEDGEHOG

replace soiled materials when necessary.

LEAVING HEDGIE AT HOME

If you are traveling, the best solution is to leave your hedgehog home in the care of a responsible person. This could be a friend, family member, or a professional pet-sitter. If you purchased your hedgehog from a breeder, you may able to board your pet with that person while you are away, or you may be able to board your hedgehog with your veterinarian.

If a friend or relative is to take care of your hedgehog, have the person come to your home so they can see beforehand everything involved in caring for your pet. Show your caretaker how to care for your hedgehog, including how to give your pet free time to run loose in a hedgehog-proof area.

Write a list of all the tasks required in caring for your hedgehog, so your caretaker won't forget what to do. Be sure to include a number where you can be reached, as well as your veterinarian's phone number and the phone number and address of a 24 hour emergency vet clinic experienced in treating hedgehogs.

If you don't have a reliable friend or relative who can care for your hedgie, consider hiring a professional pet-sitter. Most professional pet-sitters are experi-

If you are traveling, it's best to leave your hedgehog at home in the care of a responsible person. But if you must travel with your hedgie, keep him in his travel carrier at all times.

enced in caring for all kinds of pets, and most also offer other services such as taking in the mail and watering plants. To find a professional pet-sitter in your area, you can look in the phone book, search the Internet, or ask your veterinarian for a recommendation. Be sure to interview any pet-sitter you are considering and be sure he or she has a firm knowledge of how to care for hedgehogs.

You can also board your hedgie with your veterinarian, assuming your vet provides this service. Make sure your veterinarian has experience caring for hedgehogs before you entrust your pet to the vet and the hospital staff. A veterinarian specializing in exotic animals is a good start.

Nutrition and Feeding

One of the nicest aspects of owning a hedgehog is that these pets are easy to feed. Hedgehogs are insectivores, and so live well on a meat-based diet.

COMMERCIAL FOODS

Over the past few years, a number of commercial hedgehog foods have appeared on the market, making it especially easy for hedgie owners to know what to feed their pets. Most of these foods are available only through the Internet, although some specialty pet stores may carry them.

You can either feed your pet food made especially for hedgehogs or provide a high-quality, low-calorie, dry cat food. Whichever you choose, look for a product that has at least 30 percent protein and no more than 15 percent fat. (Avoid canned cat food, as this does not offer enough abrasion for the teeth and doesn't keep long once it has been put in the cage.)

When choosing food for your hedgehog, check out the ingredients on the label. You want to see whole meat or a meat meal ingredient listed in the top three ingredients. This can include chicken, lamb, or beef. Avoid products with poultry or meat or poultry by-products because these indicate a lower quality of food. You should also be sure that processed corn is not high on the list of ingredients, because your hedgie may find this item disagreeable.

African Hedgehogs need only about 30 to 70 calories per day to maintain their weight, but a hedgehog can eat 33 percent of his body weight in one sitting, if allowed. Because many hedgehogs will eat whatever is put in front of them, constant access to dry food can result in a dangerous weight

African Hedgehogs need about 30 to 70 calories per day to maintain their weight, but any hedgehog can eat 33 percent of his body weight in one sitting, if allowed.

problem. To keep your pet healthy, give him four tablespoons of dry food per day. If he gains weight on this, cut back to three tablespoons. Be sure your pet also has an exercise wheel in his cage and opportunity for exercise outside the cage.

FRESH FOODS

In addition to dry commercial hedgehog or cat food, hedgehogs need fresh foods to stay healthy and should receive treats no more than three to four times a week. You should offer your pet cooked, unseasoned chicken, tuna, liver and salmon; brewer's yeast; cooked lentils, cabbage, and cauliflower; peas and corn, either cooked or raw; and whole grain cereal cooked in meat broth. You can also offer just about any vegetable. Not all hedge-hogs will eat all vegetables, but you will quickly learn what your hedgie likes and what he doesn't.

Hedgehogs also enjoy an occasional piece of fruit. Try offering your pet a slice of apple, pear, banana, peach or plum, and see which fruit he likes. If none of these strikes his fancy, try other fruits to see which ones he prefers.

If you want to offer low-fat cottage cheese and yogurt to your hedgie as an occasional treat, you may do so. Otherwise, avoid feeding him milk products, as these are not good for his digestive system.

INSECTS

In the wild, hedgehogs hunt insects as their primary source of food. You can give your hedgehog an occasional insect as a treat to help keep him

Hedgehogs need fresh foods in addition to dry commercial hedgehog or cat food to stay healthy, and should receive treats no more than three to four times a week.

THE GUIDE TO OWNING A HEDGEHOG

Water is a crucial part of your hedgehog's diet, and should always be available to your pet. Make sure you change the water every day so it will be fresh.

entertained. Crickets and mealworms are usually the easiest insect foods to purchase, but you should only feed this to your hedgehog sparingly. One feeder insect a week is enough. Before you feed a cricket, keep it for 12 hours in a container with air holes and some commercially made cricket food, available at stores that sell live crickets. Be sure to include a slice of apple or another piece of fresh fruit or vegetable as a water supply. All of this will provide more nutrition for your hedgehog when he consumes the insect.

If you prefer to catch crawling outdoor insects for your hedgehog, be certain these bugs have not been exposed to insecticides. Don't offer spiders to your hedgehog because some species can be poisonous.

The insects African Hedgehogs prefer in the wild include beetles, ants, termites, grasshoppers, moths, centipedes, and earthworms. Offer these insects in the evening when hedgehogs most prefer to hunt.

WATER

Water is a crucial part of your hedgehog's diet, and should always be available to your pet. Change your hedgehog's water every day so it will be fresh. The water bottle in his cage should also be cleaned every day to prevent a buildup of algae and bacteria.

Always keep an eye on the water level in your hedgehog's water bottle. While hedgies don't usually drink a lot of water, they should always have an ample supply in their cage.

Handling and Training

One of the reasons hedgehogs are becoming more popular as pets is their interesting appearance. The cute face of a hedgehog, accompanied by the body of prickly quills, fascinates people. The urge to hold them is often tempered by a fear of getting poked by a spine. However, enough people

If you're worried about being pricked by one of your hedgie's quills when you first start handling him, wear a pair of thick gloves, like gardening gloves.

Speaking to your hedgehog in a soft, soothing voice will calm him and help him realize that you are a friend, not an enemy.

are willing to take the chance, evidenced by the number of people who choose to keep these animals as pets. The truth of the matter is the more you handle your hedgehog, the sooner he will bond with you.

When interacting with your hedgehog, it's important to remember that although hedgies are hunters themselves (mostly bugs), they also have a fear of being hunted. Their ability to curl into a ball to protect themselves notwithstanding, hedgehogs are easily spooked when it comes to potential predators. The result is that they often react protectively and can be quick to curl up or retreat.

For this reason, you will soon discover that the slightest wrong move can send your hedgehog scurrying to his hide box, clicking his tongue at you, or rolling into a ball. But if you move slowly, talk softly, and handle your hedgie gently, especially in the beginning, you'll find that your hedgehog will learn to trust you. He will let down his guard and start to relax. Realize that your hedgehog can switch quickly into flight mode similarly to the way most animals, and even humans, do. Don't be surprised to see him run for it and roll into a ball if something startles him.

HOW TO PICK UP A HEDGEHOG

So how do you handle an animal covered with sharp quills? It does take a little practice at first, especially if the hedgehog is less than cooperative.

If you are worried about getting poked by a quill, you can start handling your hedgehog while wearing a pair of heavy gloves. Gardening gloves work well, especially the kind used for trimming rose bushes. Take some time to keep the outside of the gloves against your skin before you handle your hedgehog. Doing so will make the gloves take on your scent and allow your pet to get used to the familiar odor.

If you are willing, you can pick your hedgehog up barehanded. If you get pricked with a spine, simply wash your hands with soap and water to avoid getting a possible allergic reaction.

First, before you reach for your hedgehog, speak to him in a soft, soothing voice. This will help calm him and help him realize you are a friend, not an enemy. Then, move your hand slowly toward him and slide your fingers underneath him where no quills can be found. You can then lift your hedgehog up slowly and cup your hands together, so he has more room to rest. Hold him against your body to give him a sense of security. Be careful not to press him too closely into your torso because you don't want to get poked.

If your hedgehog rolls into a ball, clicks his tongue at you, or tries to run away, simply put him back in his cage and try again in a few minutes after he's had a chance to calm down. It may be that your hedgehog was not socialized well when he was young and has had very little human handling. If this is the case, you will need considerable patience before you'll be able handle him. Continue to talk to him and spend time with him, and limit your handling sessions to a few minutes. Gradually earn your hedgehog's trust until he seems more comfortable when you try to handle him.

TAMING YOUR HEDGEHOG

If you purchased your hedgehog as a youngster or bought him from a breeder who socialized him when he was young, your pet is probably very tame and easy to handle. However, hedgehogs that have not been handled much while young can be truly afraid of humans when they grow up. These hedgehogs are not lost causes, however. They can still be taught to appreciate human company with knowledge and patience.

Your first step in taming your hedgehog is to let him get used to his new surroundings. Allow him a few days to get used to his new cage and the room where his cage is situated. In the meantime, be sure to reach your hands into his cage every day to give him food and water. If you move slowly and talk to him in a soothing voice while you are doing these daily chores, he will get used to your presence and learn that you aren't going to hurt him.

Your first step in taming your pet is to let him get used to his new surroundings, which include his cage and the room where his cage is located.

Hedgehogs can be trained to come when called. Your primary tool when teaching your pet to come to you is his favorite treat. Eventually, simple praise and attention will be enough reward.

Eventually, you'll notice your hedgehog becoming more comfortable around you. Instead of diving for his hide box, clicking his tongue at you, or rolling into a ball whenever you put your hand inside the cage, he'll stay out and watch you. Once this happens, you can move onto the next stage of the taming process.

While holding a small piece of unseasoned chicken or tuna, put your hand in your hedgie's cage and offer him the treat from your fingers. Once your pet starts taking the treats from you (no more than one of these treats per day, four days a week), place the treat on the palm of your hand. Your hedgie will need to crawl partway onto your hand to retrieve the treat and will learn to feel comfortable having physical contact with you. When your hedgehog is touching your hand, be sure to remain perfectly still while talking to him in a quiet, soothing voice.

When you are ready to try holding your hedgehog, follow the instructions in this chapter about handling. If your hedgehog becomes frightened and runs away from you, go back to the taming process because he needs more time to get used to you.

COMING WHEN CALLED

You won't be able to teach your hedgehog to do elaborate tricks like you might a dog, but you can train your pet to come when called, which will make living with him a whole lot easier.

First, before you can begin training your hedgehog, you need to establish a strong emotional bond between you and your pet. He must trust you completely before you can start training him.

Your primary tool when first training your hedgie to come when called is a favorite treat. Figure out which treat your hedgehog likes best and work with that. Just be sure you don't overdo it because too many treats can make your hedgehog dangerously obese.

While you'll need treats in the very beginning to teach your hedgehog what you want him to do, eventually, simple praise and attention will be enough reward for your pet.

When you first start training your hedgie, reserve treats only for this special time of the day. Do not give out treats for "free" during the training session but only when you are teaching your hedgehog to come.

Start by picking a word or phrase that you want to use as a cue for your pet. It could be "Hedgie, come!" or "Treat time!" or anything you desire, as long as the phrase is not too long. ("Hedgie, come to me and get this yummy treat!" is too long. Your hedgehog won't be able to learn this as a verbal command.)

With the treat in your hand, approach your hedgehog while he's in his cage or out in his exercise area. Say the word or phrase you have chosen as you hold the treat out to your hedgehog. Your hedgehog will probably come to you right away to get the treat. While he hasn't yet put the word or phrase together with the treat yet, he will catch on if you repeat this every day for a period of time. (The amount of time depends on your hedgehog and how fast it takes your pet to learn.) Eventually, you can eliminate the treat altogether and just give him some attention as a reward.

LITTER BOX TRAINING

Hedgehogs can be trained to use a litter box, although some are more receptive to this training than others.

If you notice that your hedgie urinates and/or defecates in the same area of his cage all the time, place a small plastic litter box in this part of his enclosure. (Litter boxes made for small pets can be purchased from pet-supply retailers.)

If your hedgeghog has been eliminating in his bedding, place some of the soiled material in the litter box to encourage him to use the container. If he continues to go there, gradually replace the bedding with a dust-free, non-clumping clay cat litter or recycled newspaper litter. Be sure that the litter you choose is free of scents or strong odors, because these can be harmful to your hedgehog's health.

You may not be able to get your hedgehog to go in the litter box when he is outside his cage, but at least having him litter box trained when he is confined will make cage cleanup easier for you.

Time for Hedgie: Grooming and Exercise

Like humans, hedgehogs need grooming and exercise to keep fit and socially pleasing—except hedgies rely on humans to ensure their well-being. Hedgies can't do it all themselves.

GROOMING YOUR HEDGEHOG
Hedgehog owners have three good reasons to groom their hedgehogs: to keep them clean, smelling fresh, and to make sure their toenails are the proper length.

Hedgehogs need grooming and exercise to stay fit and socially pleasing. They rely on humans to keep them clean and smelling fresh.

If you need to give your pet a bath, make sure you have everything within arm's reach before you start bathing him.

Bath time

Hedgehogs can sometimes get dirty and develop an odor if they have come across something foul smelling and decided to anoint themselves with it. However, even if he isn't filthy, your hedgie will do well to receive a nice, warm bath occasionally.

Before you begin bathing your hedgehog, make sure you have everything you need within arm's reach. The items you require include a towel, a soft-bristled toothbrush, and no-tears baby shampoo.

Use a kitchen sink or utility sink to bathe your hedgie. Fill the sink with about two to three inches of lukewarm water. Gently place your pet in the sink, testing the water first to make sure it's a comfortable temperature. Don't be surprised if your pet struggles. A lot of hedgehogs dislike baths and may even defecate in the water.

Using a cup, pour some of the water over your hedgehog to wet him down, avoiding getting the water in his eyes or ears. Then put some of the shampoo in your hands and rub it into a lather. Rub this lather all over your hedgehog's body, being careful to avoid his face. Use the toothbrush to rub in between his quills, making sure you get all the areas that need washing. Be sure to thoroughly wash your hedgie's feet as well.

When you are finished, use the cup

Your hedgie's nails can be clipped with human fingernail clippers or nail clippers designed for cats. The best time to trim his nails is right after his bath.

to rinse your hedgehog thoroughly. Pour clean water over his body until all the suds are gone.

Gently lift your hedgie from the sink and dry him off with the towel. Keep him in a draft- free place while he dries off.

Nail Clipping

Hedgehog nails grow at a constant rate, and if they don't wear down or get clipped on a regular basis, they can interfere with your hedgehog's ability to walk.

Chances are, you will need to trim your hedgie's toenails now and then. If you have never done this before, you may need someone to help you. You'll also need a pair of small, human fingernail clippers or toenail clippers designed for cats. Have some styptic powder handy too, in case your hedgie's toenail bleeds when you cut it.

Immediately after your hedgie's bath is the best time to trim his nails. The outer shell of the nail will be softened by the water and will be easier to cut.

Get your helper to hold the hedgie in his or her hand and allow one of the hedgie's feet to drop down through his or her fingers. Grasp the

THE GUIDE TO OWNING A HEDGEHOG

hedgehog's foot and spread his toes out by pressing on the bottom of his foot.

Look for the quick of the nail before you cut. The quick is the dark vein that extends partway through the nail. The idea is to clip the end of the nail that doesn't contain the quick. You can shine a flashlight through the nail to help you locate the quick if you are having trouble seeing it.

Trim the tip off the nail with a nip of the clippers; then move on to the next foot. If you accidentally cut into the quick, the nail will start to bleed. Dab some styptic powder on the nail and the bleeding will stop.

If your hedgie is calm and cooperative, you can go on to trim the rest of his toenails. If he struggles a lot, consider giving him a break and coming back to the rest of his nails a little later. If you are not comfortable trimming your hedgehog's toenails, ask your veterinarian to do it for you.

FREE EXERCISE

Hedgehogs who have exercise wheels in their cages have the option of "running" on the wheel 24 hours a day. But in addition to time on their wheels, hedgehogs also need supervised time outside their cages to roam free. The more supervised time you can give your hedgie outside his cage, the better. If you can only spare half an hour one day, try to give him one or two hours the next.

Hedgehogs require supervised time outside their cages. Watch over them in a small protected garden, or, for their safety, keep them inside.

Bathrooms or small, fairly empty, small rooms with a door are good places to set aside as hedgehog roaming zones.

Why is it important to supervise your hedgie during his exercise time? So he won't get into trouble. Hedgehogs can be great escape artists and have a way of finding trouble in the most unlikely places.

Good places to set aside as hedgehog roaming zones are bathrooms or fairly empty, small rooms with a door. You can also get a plastic swimming pool made for children to use for playtime, although it should be deep so your hedgehog can't easily climb out.

Equip your hedgie's play area with his favorite toys, such as empty toilet paper rolls, rubber balls, and assorted cat toys. If your hedgie is the playful type, you'll be in for a treat as you watch him play with some of these items during his outside-the-cage time.

HEDGEHOG PROOFING

If you opt to give your hedgehog a room to roam in during his exercise time, you should hedgehog proof it first to ensure that he can't get into trouble.

Begin by getting down on all fours and looking at the room from your hedgie's point of view. Keep an eye out for electrical and telephone cords that your pet may be able to reach and chew on.

Also look for small crevices where your hedgie can hide. These can be in the wall, in a water heater, in furniture—think like a hedgehog, and be creative. You will need to plug up any spot you find that might prove tempting to your hedgie.

Bathrooms are often good places for hedgehogs to use for exercise time, although they can also hold some hazards. Make sure the toilet bowl lid is closed, and look for holes in the wall around pipes or anywhere else your hedgie can hide. Keep houseplants out of reach, and make sure the sink and bathtub are drained of water. Also remember to make sure the room you choose for your hedgie's exercise is free from other pets who might harass your hedgehog during his free time.

If you have the urge to give your hedgehog the run of the house, consider getting him a hamster exercise ball. You can put your hedgehog in one of these large, clear, plastic balls, and your pet can run around the house safely

To hedgehog proof a room, get down on all fours, so you have your pet's point of view, and look for anything your pet might chew, as well as small crevices where he might hide.

If you want to give your hedgie the run of your home, consider getting him a hamster exercise ball that he can run around in.

while confined within. If you opt for this method of exercise for your hedgehog, make sure the dog and cat are not in the house while your hedgie is running around in his ball. Your other pets are likely to think your hedgehog is a toy and will scare him if they start chasing him.

Wherever you let your hedgehog roam, be careful when you are walking around the room while your pet is loose. Hedgehogs move quickly and can easily get underfoot. The last thing you want to do is step on your hedgehog while he is out getting his exercise.

Health Care

Hedgehogs are relatively easy to keep healthy if you feed them the right diet and provide them with a clean cage, exercise, and good ventilation. Hedgehogs do get sick sometimes, though, despite your best efforts, and may require a trip to the veterinarian.

Hedgehogs are relatively easy to keep healthy if they have the right diet, exercise, a clean cage, and good ventilation.

Find a veterinarian who treats hedgehogs before your pet needs help. References are available from pet stores, breeders, rescue groups, and even veterinary teaching facilities.

Remember that you may spend more on vet bills than you actually spent on your hedgehog, but if you consider your pet a member of the family, you won't base his worth on his monetary value. Remember: Your hedgehog is completely dependent on you for care, and that includes veterinary care if he gets sick.

CHOOSING A VETERINARIAN

Don't wait for your hedgehog to get sick to find a veterinarian. Vets who know how to treat hedgehogs are few and far between, and it will take you some time to locate one in your area. Do this before your pet needs help, so you will know whom to turn to when something goes wrong.

Over the last 20 years or so, a large number of veterinarians have become interested in treating "exotics"—animals like birds, reptiles, rabbits, rodents, and hedgehogs. Although research in diseases that affect these animals is lagging behind research for cats and dogs, veterinarians who specialize in exotic pets are becoming more knowledgeable about caring for these creatures as a result of experience and continuing education.

Start by looking for a vet in your area who treats exotics. Begin by asking other hedgehog owners in your area for a referral. Word of mouth is often the best way to choose a veterinarian. If you got your pet from a rescue group or breeder, ask these people for the name of a vet who is good with hedgehogs. If you purchased your pet from a pet store, ask for a hedgehog vet referral from the pet store staff.

If you don't know anyone in your area who has a hedgehog but are fortunate enough to live near a veterinary teaching facility (like a university that grants veterinary degrees), contact the school and find out if they offer veterinary services to hedgehog owners.

Another option is to contact a local ferret organization and ask for a vet-erinarian. Vets who treat ferrets often treat hedgehogs as well.

Your last resort is to look in your local phone directory and seek out vets who advertise that they specialize in exotics.

If you have to use this last method, call a few of the vets and ask some questions. Find out if they treat hedgehogs, and ask how long they have been caring for this species. If one vet seems more knowledgeable about hedgehogs than the others, make an appointment to bring your hedgie in for a checkup.

It's a good idea to take your hedgehog for a regular exam each year, so your vet can take a look at your pet

It's a good idea for your hedgehog to have a regular exam every year, so your vet can look at your pet and make sure all is well.

and make sure all is well. At the very least, keep the veterinarian's number accessible so that, in the event of an urgent situation, you can contact him or her quickly.

If your veterinarian does not provide 24-hour emergency service, ask her for a referral to an emergency hospital that treats hedgehogs, in case you need help with your pet after hours or on the weekends. Put the number in a prominent place so you will have access to it when you need it.

HEDGEHOG HEALTH

Most of what we know about hedgehogs and what ails them comes from the experiences of breeders and rescuers who come into contact with greater numbers of these small animals. As it turns out, many of the problems that afflict other mammals also affect hedgehogs.

In order to determine if your hedgie is not feeling well, it helps to know what a healthy hedgehog looks like. Healthy hedgehogs have bright, alert expressions, plenty of energy, and firm stools. The signs that your hedgehog is sick may include one or more of these symptoms: lethargy and a reluctance to move; a dull expression; weight loss; discharge from the eyes or nose; loose stools; panting or labored breathing; or paralysis. If your pet shows any one of these signs, he needs immediate veterinary care. Don't wait to see if your pet gets bet-

Most of what is known about hedgehogs and what ails them comes from the experiences of breeders and rescuers, who come into contact with many of these small animals.

Healthy hedgehogs have bright, alert expressions, and plenty of energy. Signs of illness include lethargy, a dull expression, weight loss, panting, or labored breathing.

ter; hedgehogs can go downhill very quickly, and you may lose your pet if you hesitate to get help.

PREVENTATIVE CARE

As with all mammals, including humans, the secret to good health is prevention. Do everything you can to keep your pet healthy. It's much easier to keep a hedgehog in good shape than it is to try to fix a problem that resulted from improper care.

The best way to keep your hedgie healthy is to follow the advice for housing, feeding, and general care outlined in this book. In particular, make sure your hedgehog always has a clean cage. Remove urine-soiled bedding and feces as soon as you can and wash his water bowl and food

Feed your hedgehog the best food you can afford, and don't let him live in unsanitary conditions.

bowls every day. Don't let your hedgehog live in unsanitary conditions. If you do, you are asking for trouble.

Feed your hedgehog the best food you can afford. Skimping on the quality of food now can result in veterinary bills later. Be sure the food you give your hedgie is fresh. Don't be tempted to buy large quantities of dry food because it's less expensive. The food will lose its nutritional value over time, and your hedgehog won't be getting the nutrients he needs to stay healthy.

Make sure your hedgehog has a constant supply of fresh water. Water is vital to maintaining his good health.

OBSERVING YOUR HEDGEHOG

Hedgehogs are happy creatures, but only when they are healthy. Keep a close eye on your pet and watch his behavior. The way he acts is the best clue to how he is feeling. Get to know what your hedgehog is like when he is feeling good. If his behavior suddenly changes, something may be wrong.

Look for physical evidence of a problem, too. If your hedgehog has a lump, crusty skin, an abscess, soft stool, discharge from the ears, a runny nose, or anything else going on with his body that is out of the ordinary, call your veterinarian.

HEDGEHOG AILMENTS

Some of the more commonly seen hedgehog illnesses and conditions are listed below. These descriptions can give you an idea of what kind of problems you may see on your hedgie. Be aware, however, that your veterinarian is the best person to diagnose these problems, and he or she is the only one who can truly help your pet.

Soft Stools

The hedgehog suffering from soft stool has feces that are soft, often green in color, and particularly foul smelling. If the problem persists for more than 24 hours, it's a good idea to take your hedgie to the vet.

Some causes of soft stool include eating something that disagrees with the hedgie's digestive system, bacterial infection, and parasites.

Eye Problems

Hedgehogs have eyes that tend to protrude, therefore causing them to be susceptible to injury. If your hedgie is holding his eye shut, is pawing repeatedly as his eye, and/or experiences tearing from the eye, he may have an irritation. Take him to the vet, so he or she can determine the exact cause of the problem. The irritation may be caused by something as simple as a piece of dust, or it can be the result of a scratch to the eye or an infection. Whatever the cause of the irritation, your vet can prescribe medication to help your hedgehog heal.

Skin Problems

Hedgehogs are prone to several dif-

Know what your hedgie is like when he is feeling well. Something is wrong if his behavior suddenly changes.

ferent types of skin problems. Fungus is a problem that can make a hedgie's skin raw and scaly between the quills. If you suspect your hedgie is suffering from skin fungus, take your pet to a veterinarian right away. Your vet will diagnose the problem with a skin culture, and give you a prescription to treat the problem.

Dermatitis is another problem that affects hedgehogs and should be treated by a vet. Scaly, itchy skin is a sign of this malady.

Skin mites can also infest hedgehogs, as can fleas, causing itching and irritation on the skin. These parasites can only be eliminated with the help of medication prescribed by a veterinarian.

Internal Parasites

Hedgehogs are susceptible to a number of internal parasites, including fluke trematode and capillaria erinacea. Each of these parasites can cause serious problems with your hedgehog's digestive system. Symptoms of these diseases include soft, green, foul-smelling stool, a lack of energy, a poor appearance, and weight loss.

When you first get your hedgehog, it's a good idea to have him checked for internal parasites by your veterinarian. This involves a fecal test, where your pet's stool will be examined for signs of infection. The treatment will depend on which parasite, if any, the veterinarian finds in the exam.

Keep a close eye on your hedgehog's mouth and take a look inside it whenever you can to see if any tooth problems are developing.

Tooth Problems

Over the course of their lives, some hedgehogs develop tooth problems, such as missing or worn-down teeth and abscesses. Missing or worn teeth require a softer diet, so the hedgehog can eat properly without being in too much pain. In most cases, dry cat food dampened with water is soft enough for the hedgie to swallow. Abscesses, on the other hand, can be dangerous and require care from a veterinarian. The abscessed tooth my have to be removed and the hedgie placed on antibiotics.

Keep a close eye on your hedgehog's mouth and take a look inside it whenever you can to see if any tooth problems may be developing.

Respiratory Infections

Hedgehog owners need to always be on guard against respiratory infections in their pets. Pneumonia is one disease that is often seen in hedgies, along with other kinds of bacterial infections that attack the animal's airways. The lungworm, a parasite that lives in the lungs, can also cause respiratory distress.

Signs of respiratory distress include a runny or crusty nose, raspy breathing, and coughing. If untreated, this can progress into lethargy, loss of appetite, and, ultimately, death.

Respiratory diseases can be treated successfully with antibiotics administered by your veterinarian, assuming the ailment is treated early. Hedgehogs can go downhill quickly when they are afflicted with a respiratory illness, so it's important to take your pet to the vet at the very first sign of respiratory problem.

Ear Troubles

Hedgehogs are prone to getting ear mites, parasites that can cause ear irritation and a nasty-smelling buildup inside your pet's ears. Your veterinarian will need to diagnose and treat the problem. Because fungus can also affect a hedgehog's ears, it's vital that your vet determine the cause of the irritation.

Wobbly Hedgehog Syndrome

Many people who breed or rescue hedgehogs know all too well about a tragic neurological condition called Wobbly Hedgehog Syndrome (WHS). Wobbly Hedgehog Syndrome is a chronic, progressive paralysis that ultimately results in a hedgehog that cannot walk. The problem usually begins in the hindquarters and is characterized by a wobbly gait. Nearly complete paralysis is often the end result. It can happen to hedgehogs of any age and is believed to be inherited.

Currently, no cure exists for Wobbly Hedgehog Syndrome, which is one reason why it's important to buy a hedgehog from a reputable breeder who has healthy animals.

Fortunately, you can provide supportive care for a hedgehog diagnosed with this condition. By assisting the hedgehog in accessing food, feeding good-quality food, and providing accommodations that make getting around easier, you can help him live a longer, happier life.

Before you assume your hedgehog is suffering from Wobbly Hedgehog Syndrome, take your pet to a vet for a definitive diagnosis. A number of other problems can mimic this condition, including nutritional problems, strokes, tumors, bacterial infections, and injuries.

Cancer

Unfortunately, hedgehogs are prone to cancerous tumors. Examine your hedgehog's body on a regular basis and keep an eye out for lumps, bumps, and skin tumors. The most likely place to find a visible malignant tumor is in the mammary glands or on the jaw. Internal tumors sometimes develop on the liver, lungs and spleen.

If you suspect your hedgehog has a tumor or if he isn't feeling well, take him to a veterinarian right away. The earlier the diagnosis of cancer, the greater the chances of helping your pet.

HEDGEHOG FIRST AID

In case of an emergency, your first priority should be to get your hedgehog to a veterinarian right away. However, you can take some actions to slow bleeding and provide temporary care as you are on the way to the vet.

Although you can administer first aid to your hedgie, in case of emergency, your first priority should be to get your hedgehog to a veterinarian right away.

Making a First-Aid Kit

First off, you'll need to put together a hedgehog first-aid kit to use in case your hedgie runs into trouble and needs immediate help before he sees a vet.

The following items should be included in your first-aid kit.

- Cotton balls
- Small towel
- Antiseptic scrub
- Gauze
- Antibiotic ointment
- Styptic powder
- Scissors

You can keep all these items in a box designated for your hedgehog. Know where it is so you can find it quickly should you need to attend to your pet in a hurry.

SAYING GOODBYE

The day will come when you will have to say goodbye to your sweet, little hedgehog. Your pet may die from old age or succumb to a disease or condition despite all your attempts to save him. In some cases, euthanasia is an option some hedgehog owners may consider if pain or illness becomes too great.

Euthanasia is the veterinary process of taking an animal's life. This is done in situations where the animal is beyond hope and in great pain or distress. It is also done in cases where the cost of treating the pet is way beyond the means of the pet's owner.

It's important to take your pet to the vet at the very first sign of illness. As with humans, diseases and other conditions in hedgehogs are easier to cure or manage if caught early.

When veterinarians euthanize a hedgehog, they inject substantial quantities of a barbiturate into the animal's blood stream. This drug causes brain function to stop almost immediately, causing the hedgehog to become unconscious. After this happens, the hedgehog stops breathing and the heart stops beating.

When a hedgehog is euthanized, he does not feel any pain, or even fear, from what we can tell. The sensation of euthanasia is simply that of falling into a deep sleep.

In some situations, choosing euthanasia is the kindest, most caring option for a hedgie who is suffering great pain and has lost his quality of life. This is a very personal decision, and you should discuss this issue with your veterinarian.

The Grieving Process

People are often amazed at how devastated they become when they lose a beloved pet. Many people assume that strong feelings of grief should only be present with the loss of a human being. However, the human heart does not qualify love according to species. For many people, the loss of a pet is nearly as devastating as the loss of a human being.

Be prepared to feel very powerful feelings of loss when you say goodbye to your hedgehog. A variety of emotions will overtake you, but, eventually, you will reach a stage of acceptance, and your broken heart will slowly begin to heal.

Unfortunately, those who do not have pets or don't have strong bonds with their animals do not often understand the grief that pet lovers experience when they lose a cherished pet. The good news is other devoted pet owners *do* understand what you are feeling, and can provide considerable support in your time of need.

Another option is to contact a pet grief hotline. A number of veterinary schools and other associations provide this service for free to those who have just lost a pet. Pet grief counselors will talk to you about your pet, and how you are feeling. Their sympathy can do wonders to help you heal.

THE NEXT STEP

It may take a bit of time, but, eventually, you will probably want to give a home to another one of these delightful pets. While a new hedgehog can never replace the one you have lost, giving a home to another hedgie can help mend your heart while giving you a new friend to love.

Resources

ORGNIZATIONS

A Spiny Place Hedgehog Rescue
194 Rolling Hills Drive
Boone, NC 28607
Phone: (828) 262-0804
E-mail: info@aspinyplace.com
Website: www.aspinyplace.com

Hedgehog Welfare Society
5308 21st Ave SW #403
Seattle, WA 98106
E-mail: info@hedgehogwelfare.org
Website: www.hedgehogwelfare.org

The International Hedgehog Association
P.O. Box 10601
Divide, CO 80814
Phone: (250) 499-5143
Fax: (250) 499-5143
E-mail: info@hedgehogclub.com
Website: www.hedgehogclub.com

INTERNET RESOURCES

The Flash and Thelma Memorial Hedgehog Rescue
E-mail: MGSpikers@aol.com
www.hedgieflash.org

Hedgehog Central
This website provides detailed information on care, rescue, and registering your hedgehog, as well as a veterinarian list and links to other hedgehog websites.
www.hedgehogcentral.com

Hedgehog Valley
E-mail: hhvalley@yahoo.com
www.hedgehogvalley.com

Hedgies.com
www.hedgies.com

Northwest Hedgehogs: Hedgehog News
www.hhnews.com/hedgies

Pet Finder
Petfinder.com is an online, searchable database of over 100,000 animals that need homes from over 5,000 animal shelters and adoption organizations across the USA and Canada. www.petfinder.org

PetsHub Hedgehogs
www.petshub.com/hedgehogs

Petswelcome.com
This website features listings of hotels for pet owners.
www.petswelcome.com

VETERINARY RESOURCES

The American Veterinary Medical Association
1931 North Meacham Road, Suite 100
Schaumburg, IL 60173
Phone: (847) 925-8070
Fax: (847) 925-1329
E-mail: avmainfo@avma.org
www.avma.org

EMERGENCY SERVICES

ASPCA National Animal Poison Control Center
1717 S. Philo, Suite 36
Urbana, IL 61802
1-888-426-4435
www.aspca.org

Animal Poison Hotline
(888) 232-8870

Index

Photo Credits

Ralph Lermayer: 1, 5, 7, 8, 9, 11, 14, 17, 21, 23, 27, 30, 31, 37, 39, 42, 45, 46, 47, 48, 49, 50, 54, 60
Isabelle Francais: 4, 15, 24, 26, 28, 35, 36, 38, 41, 44, 51, 61
Joan Balzarini: 56
Dave Dube: 55
M. Gilroy: 58